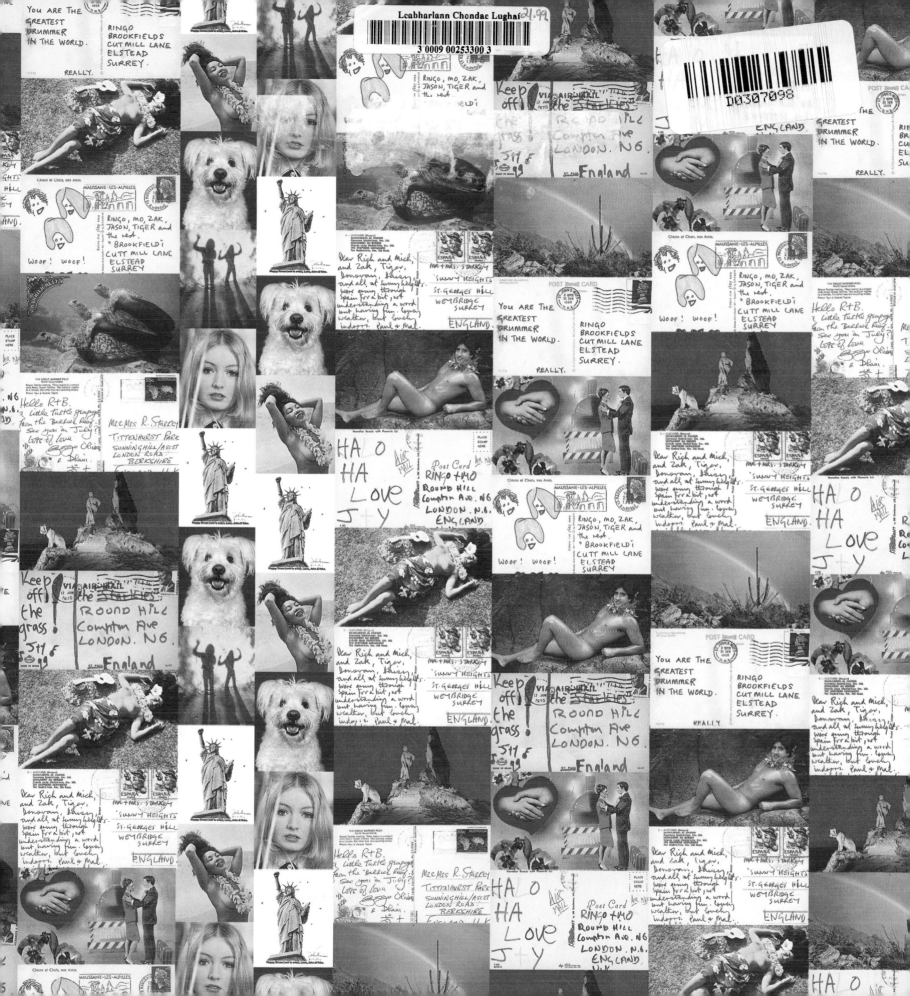

POSTCARDS FROM THE BOYS

POSTCARDS FROM THE BOYS
RINGO STARR

Featuring postcards sent by John Lennon,
Paul McCartney and George Harrison

CASSELL
ILLUSTRATED

This edition first published in Great Britain in 2004 by
Cassell Illustrated, a member of Octopus Publishing Group Limited
2-4 Heron Quays
London E14 4JP

A CIP catalogue record for this book is available from the British Library.

ISBN: 1 84403 278 7

This book first appeared as a signed, limited edition,
designed and produced by Genesis Publications Limited.
www.genesis-publications.com

'A lot of other people know more about my life than I do' writes Ringo Starr here.

He may well be right. Many others' lifetimes have gone into chronicling those of The Beatles. Countless hours of research, analysis and debate have consumed amateur myth-makers and professional pedants alike. Such has been the Fab Four's impact on western society, the facts of their lives have become public property.

We know, for instance, that they meditated with the Maharishi, and that they played their last concert on the roof of the Apple building. And we know that in the final years, recording sessions could be tense, fractious affairs.

But lives are more than a series of facts cemented together into a proper order. For all the factual breeze-blocks of the Beatles' lives we piece together, we only ever see the outside of the building. We rarely get to peek inside the rooms where John, Paul, George and Ringo played together, laughed, bickered and forged relationships stronger then mere friendships. In this book, Ringo opens 51 small windows into those rooms.

On the following pages are a selection of postcards sent to him by 'the boys.' Accompanying them are Ringo's comments; whatever thoughts and memories came to him as he thumbed through this collection. The well-known stories do not need to be re-told; as Ringo observes, 'it's in *all* the books.' Instead these little windows throw light in unexpected places.

There are the three sent by Paul between 27-31 January, 1969, while the band were finishing the troubled recording of *Let It Be*; one is a cryptic apology from 'Mr B Lumpy' while another, sent the day after the band's performance on the roof of Apple Studios states simply: 'You are the greatest drummer in the world. Really.' There's news from the band's retreat in Rishikesh – Ringo had returned home early – that John and George had managed seven hours of meditation; Paul and his girlfriend of the time, Jane Asher, two and a half. And that the Maharishi was planning to build a new swimming pool.

Less than a month after the initiation of court proceedings to bring about a legal dissolution of The Beatles, on a card dated January 21, 1971, John has written simply and despondently, 'Who'd have thought it would come to this?' By the late Seventies, when Ringo's solo career was – in his words – 'turning to hell,' John is suggesting Blondie's 'Heart Of Glass' is 'the type of stuff y'all should do.'

One card, bearing just a cartoon and the legend, 'Hiya Toots', stirs Ringo's memories of a fireworks party he and John gave for their kids. Another reminds him of quitting The Beatles in 1968. As the rest of the band got on with mixing *The White Album* he flew to Sardinia where he spent an afternoon on Peter Sellers' yacht and wrote 'Octopus's Garden'. When he returned ten days later, it was partly as a result – Ringo has since revealed – of several telegrams and postcards from the boys he received in that time.

The postcards themselves range from the bizarre to the banal; from naked Hawaiian beauties to cats playing with balls and a photo of Scotland's Campbeltown high street. On them the correspondents have scribbled haikus, drawings, odd references to long-forgotten private jokes and wishes of love and happiness for a good friend.

In fact, this is the most revealing aspect of these cards: that no matter what we might have read, no matter what we've been told and no matter how it sometimes might have appeared to the world at large, John, Paul, George and Ringo retained a familial bond throughout all and everything. They stayed friends, even if they couldn't stay as The Beatles

As Ringo writes: 'It didn't matter what people's perceptions of us were, you can see from these cards that there's still a lot of contact, a lot of thought. The relationship never went away.'

RB Elson

From Paul, and Mal Evans. This has got to be one of our oldest cards. Zak was our only child at this point. November '66. We moved to Weybridge in '65. This is probably Paul's last holiday with Mal. He was killed in the Seventies. Mal was great – the gentle giant. I first met him in The Cavern. He was a part-time bouncer and worked for the Post Office as an electrician. Neil Aspinall needed some help with the equipment and Mal was always this friendly, big guy and so we got him involved. That's all we ever had, Neil and Mal – what a team – thanks!

5 — AMEYUGO (Burgos)
MONUMENTO AL PASTOR
Carretera Madrid-Irún, Km. 308.
MONUMENT AU BERGER
Grande route Madrid-Irún, Km. 308.
THE SHEPHERD MONUMENT
The Madrid-Irún, Km. 308 Road.

Dear Rich and Mich,
and Zak, Tiger,
Donovan, Daisy,
and all at 'sunny heights'.
Were going through
Spain for a bit, not
understanding a word
but having fun. Lousy
weather, but lovely
indoors. Paul + Mal.
Available for social functions.

Postal Éter. Burgos

MR. + MRS. STARKEY
'SUNNY HEIGHTS'
ST. GEORGES HILL
WEYBRIDGE
SURREY
ENGLAND.

Depósito Legal B. 25.855-66

These are our early days at St George's Hill. The thing about being in Weybridge in that house was that I bought half of the building firm that was working on it because I thought they'd get the job done much faster. Not a chance in hell! Builders do things in their own good time. And the foreman would cook Maureen and I dinner because she couldn't cook.

St George's Hill. I lived there until '69. John and I were both in St George's Hill and George was in Esher and so the three of us were in the same area. Paul was the man about town at this time. He liked to take his dog for walks on Hampstead Heath and places like that. I mainly saw John in that period because we lived a couple of blocks from each other. We used to spend practically every weekend together. We'd edit 8mm film and have fun – sometimes hysterical fun. I'd walk home. John had Julian and I had Zak so we'd try and do the fatherly things. We'd try and do manly things too; we'd go to the pub and bring Maureen and Cynthia a Babycham or something – a real Liverpool attitude.

One Bonfire Night that we had at my place, John and I decided to show our kids
(they must have been two and three) some fireworks. We went and bought all
these fizzy ones. We'd smoked a lot of herbalized stuff so we didn't want anything
really loud. We were doing this whole set up and sitting around, relaxing a little
and we went outside to give the babies this big show and everything we bought
just exploded! Exploded! What the kids must have thought, I don't know because
the grown-ups were going 'Ow! Ow! Aaaagh!' We were so shocked we had to go
back inside.

And that's what makes our children what they are today

This is a very old card. I think this is probably the only card I've got from John and Cyn. And Victor Spinetti. On one holiday – Maureen, John, Cyn and I went to Tobago and John had just got contact lenses and he dropped one; it came out in the swimming pool. We spent about three hours in the pool looking for this damn contact! We didn't find it obviously.

Anyway, that's nice to have. Marrakech. Victor and John were friendly enough to go on holiday. John liked to have Welsh people around him.

UMAPATI SHANKER

S.S. BRIJBASI & SONS
MATHURA U.P

COPYRIGHTS
RESERVED

It's a novel from John. We're still in Weybridge, '68. It's great, he's saying he's got about two LPs worth of songs. It's like a letter. This is a month after I'd left the band for a while. We did some tracks. We'd all been recording. It's in *all* the books — it wasn't happening so I went on holiday, thanks to Peter Sellers, to Sardinia and borrowed his yacht. It's incredible how some good can come out of turmoil because that's where I wrote 'Octopus's Garden'. We asked for fish and chips and the guy gave us squid. I said, 'What the hell is that?' and then he told me this whole story about octopuses and how they put stones around themselves in the ocean. So I got my three chords on guitar and wrote 'Octopus's Garden'.

Paul and Jane in Rishikesh. We had to leave the others there because we had children at home but we also left because we only planned to go for two weeks in the first place. Maureen had this fly/moth phobia and to be in the jungle of India didn't help! But it's incredible – John and George got up to seven hours of meditation. Paul got to two and a half. We never got that far – an hour at the most. Mia Farrow was great – she was there too. This was a really good time because it relieved all that pressure of being The Beatles.

I first heard about the Maharishi after I returned from the hospital when our son Jason was born. There was a message from John and from George who'd just been to hear him and they said, 'We're going to Wales, you've got to come with us.' So we got the train which poor Cyn missed.

Everything here is still going well, except we miss you both. John and George have each done 7 hours, but we've only managed 2½ so far, but we're hoping to do longer ones before we leave. The weather is getting hotter, and there have been complaints about mosquitoes, so Mo isn't the only one. Mia left yesterday and Mal today — latest news is that Maharishi's building a swimming pool! Much love, Paul v Jane.

MR. & MRS.
R. STARKEY,
SUNNY HEIGHTS,
ST. GEORGE'S HILL,
WEYBRIDGE,
SURREY,
ENGLAND.

The Maharishi had no idea who we were and thought we were other travellers, devotees, whatever. As soon as he found out, he thought it would be good if we did a world tour — and we weren't touring then! — to pass on his message.

The sad thing about going to Wales was that was when Brian died. Later we went to Rishikesh and it was amazing. It was always difficult for me because I had this food situation so I always took a suitcase full of clothes and a suitcase full of beans so I could eat! Now I take all those great protein bars. There was so much good music in Rishikesh. A lot of the guys wrote some good songs there — if nothing else, that was well worth it. In many ways it was also our first experience of being left alone, although the press caught up with us and photographed us leaving. But we did have plenty of time on our own. The bathroom was full of scorpions — these are just flash memories — you had to make a lot of noise before you went in. And that was that. I'm still glad I went and feel so blessed I met the Maharishi — he gave me a mantra that no-one can take away and I still use it.

Another fun card from 'you-know-who'. This is an older card from when we were living in the house I acquired when I made *The Magic Christian* movie with Peter Sellers. The deal was I got some money and his house! We didn't live there for long – we were only there nine months or a year. It was just too far out of London in those days. I sold it on to Stephen Stills. But great little drawings – well done! It has to be '69.

Paul was always very good at postcarding. And they *all* knew that I love postcards. Even to this day, when people say, 'Oh I'm going to such and such,' I always say, 'Oh send me a card.' I like to get them, but I'm not the best at sending them. I usually write them and bring them home and post them. You know when you just don't get around to it.

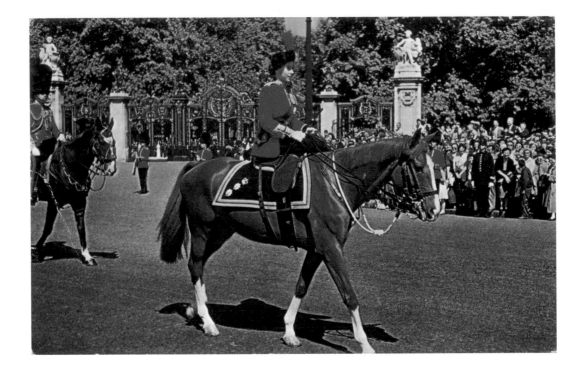

There's Her Majesty. I'm not really into Her Majesty anymore I'm afraid.

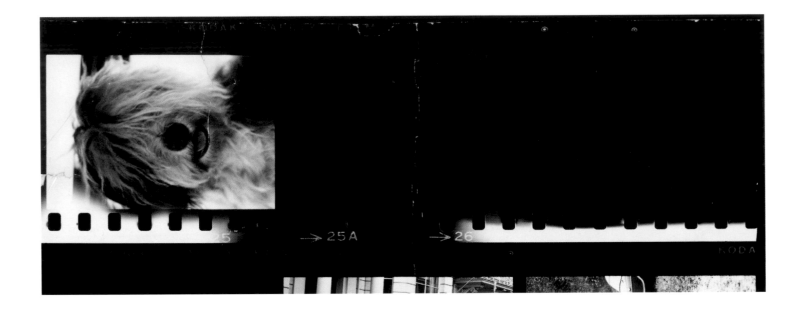

This is Martha my dear, the dog.

Another little drawing so we know it's from Paul.

Coldstream Guardsman:
Windsor Castle

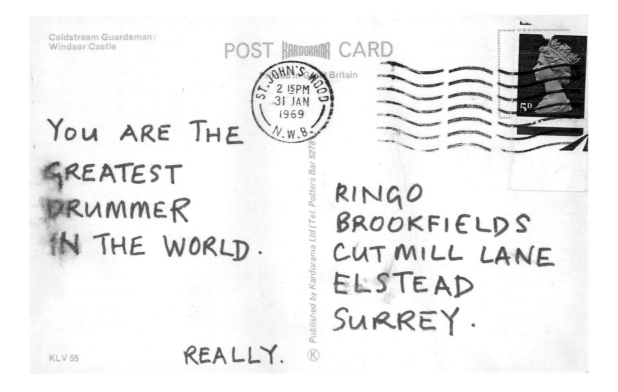

This is after the *White Album*. I thought life was hell during this period. After I walked out I kept getting these postcards – telegrams actually – from John and George: 'Come on home! You're the best!' And when I did come back, George had the whole studio decorated in flowers. It was just a beautiful moment. You know, you go through those moments in your life when things are crazy. And so I left. So Paul's just making up for lost time here. He's a year late though!

Every time I went for a cup of tea, he was on the drums!

VALENTINE'S
"VALUXE"

PUBLISHED BY VALENTINE & SONS LTD., DUNDEE & LONDON

PRINTED IN
GT. BRITAIN

5D

you GOT
THAT
SOMETHING

Except for a nother.
Fanny Brice and Barbara Streisand.

RINGO + MO
BROOKLANDS
CUT MILL LANE
ELSTEAD
SURREY.

Prince Andrew and Prince Edward in the
Oak Dining Room, Windsor Castle.
PHOTO BY STUDIO LISA.

XT.19R

It's from Paul. What was happening in my life here? Do you know?

From Paul, I think. Nothing to say but it's okay.

Dear Sir,
mr B. Lumpy.
of Oniston on Wey
Cathletown.
    Arston.
Begs your
Pardon.   ♡

MR JEREMY FISHER from the book
by Beatrix Potter
© Frederick Warne & Co Ltd, London and New York

POSTCARD

Printed in Great Britain

ADDRESS

5D

To/
BIG
BUILD ME UP
WHISKERS GALORE
BROOKFIELDS
CUT MILL LANE
ELSTEAD
SURREY .

Another great card from Paul. 1969 – by now everything was tough except the
moments when we played and that was the saving grace. Once the music started
we were always okay because we still did our best. Then afterwards there would
be lots of heated discussions. Maybe this is before we had the big meeting at
Brookfields where we asked George to come back to The Beatles after he'd left
when Paul had really, *really* pissed him off at Twickenham.

From Paul, Linda and Heather. This is great! A bit of artwork here. 'We Send All Our Love.' These are little art pieces in themselves.

That's the thing now. A lot of other people know more about my life than I do. Some people, even though they were smoking 'Jamaican brand' cigarettes all the time, remember it all.

Those were the days. 'Anniversity' — what the hell could Paul be saying? I was working on *Sentimental Journey* at this point. That was great because it was after the break-up. What was I going to do? I called George Martin and said, 'I'm going to do an album of standards that will get me out of bed, out of the house and get me back on my feet.'

I chose all the songs I was brought up with; that my mother sang, my step-father sang, my aunties, my uncles, the neighbours – everybody was singing them – you *had* to have a song in Liverpool. It was just somewhere for me to start. It did everything it needed to do for me. It was great having Quincy Jones on it. George Martin did a great job. And now they're *all* doing albums like that. This one did well for me. The thing was, after I made that album, these people flew me to Vegas because they were thinking, 'Oh, now he can play Vegas!' I went to see Elvis there actually. And that was good. But I just knew at that time, that was not what I wanted to do. I did not want to wear a bow tie but, because the video we made for it had me with the bow tie and the dancing girls, they just dived in and thought that was me now. Then I went and made the country album, but that's another story.

Stampato in Italia – Importé D'Italie – Printed in Italy

Ringo | Mo | Jr. | JF.

Brookfields

Cut (the wise cracks)
Mill Lane
Elstead Surrey
worry

Cecami

839

Riproduzione vietata

From Paul and Linda. Nice picture! Those guys had a lot of holidays!

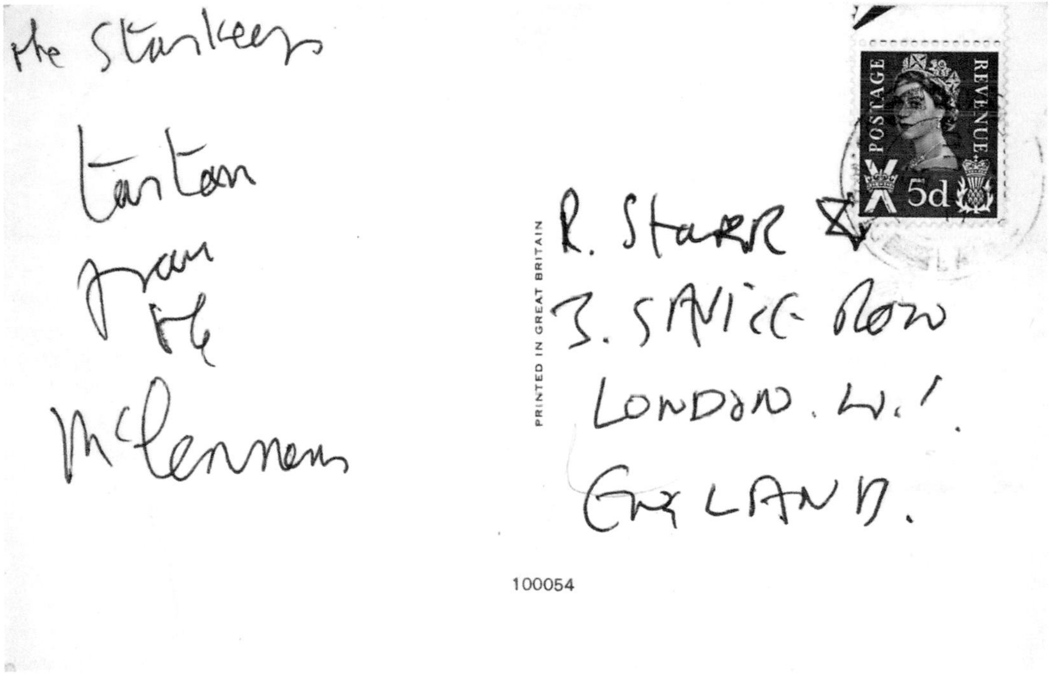

the Starkeys

tartan

from

Me

McLennen

R. Starr ☆

3. Savile Row

London. W.1.

England.

PRINTED IN GREAT BRITAIN

100054

All to Savile Row! Don't quite know where I was living.

Dear Ringo & Mo & Zak & Jason

Hello

John & Yoko
Darlin + Ringold

You See MORE in a
Harvey Barton
VIEWCARD

PRINTED IN ENGLAND

ARWISGIAD EI UCHELDER BRENHINOL TYWYSOG CYMRU YNG NGHAERNARFON AR ORFFENNAF 1af 1969.
INVESTITURE OF H.R.H. THE PRINCE OF WALES AT CAERNARVON ON JULY 1st 1969.

ACKNOWLEDGEMENT:- COLOUR STUDY BY GODFREY ARGENT, CAMERA PRESS, LONDON.

TYWYN
6 -PM
23 JNE
1969
MERIONE

MR & MRS Ringo Starkey

c/o Peter Brown

3. SAVILE ROW

LONDON . W.1,

ENGLAND

It's the young Prince. This is '69 – before Lee was born. The future *what*! God
save the Queen, if you know what I mean. We don't really need a king.

Scotland the Brave. As a child I never went there. I went to Seaforth and to New Brighton and to Sunderland to Aunt Evie and Uncle Jim's.

I cycled to North Wales once on a bike – an old Raleigh which my mum got me – with a group of kids. Before that, we used to walk everywhere. I got back and realised I'd never be doing a long cycle ride again ever. My arse was so sore.

THE KINGDOM *of* DENMARK *Copenhagen*

1970 and all the mail is going to Peter Brown in Savile Row.

John was absent from the recording of *I Me Mine* which was around this time. The original track was just George and me and he played Hammond.

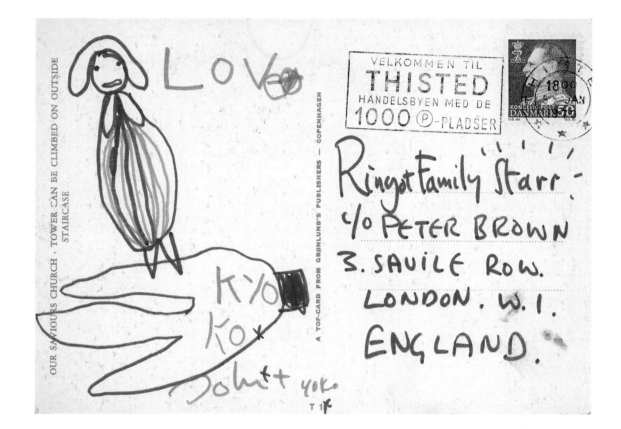

The postcards from all over the world show that the four of us were always travelling. I went to Denmark eight or nine times, more than Sweden or Finland or any of the other places. Denmark seemed to be the place to go and hang out. I was always going to Germany. I had to keep travelling. I went to Barbados like a hundred times.

Once Harry Nilsson and I ended up in Austria looking for Johann Strauss! We met Robert Altman instead and finished up in a hotel in Denmark and I believe we had a heated discussion halfway through dinner – him, Harry and I – and the end result was I ended up in Greece with somebody, in Athens!

Another one from John and Yoko. Looks like Willie Nelson cooking breakfast after the IRS had finished with him.

John was sending back his MBE to the Queen. Well he'd made a statement. Good on him. I was doing that, he was doing this. That's how it was. He got a bee in his bonnet and sent it back.

This is probably the oldest one from John and Yoko. Now we've moved to Highgate.
We moved there in 1970.

The Primal Scream thing with John and Yoko around this period was very interesting
for the rest of us. They'd been before because I remember them going to see Janov
when we were The Beatles. The Primal Scream concept is letting some emotions out
and getting to others that you've buried all these years.

WHALE BREACH
All the animals in the Whale Tank breach — that is, they leap high in the air and then crash full body length against the surface of the huge salt water pool. This is a natural behavior in the ocean used by the animals to knock barnacles from their bodies and to scratch.

did you know we were the youngest bores of the year!?!?

love John yoko

the Starkies.
Round Hill
Compton Ave. N.G.
England LONDON
GRate BRITON.

I can say this now (if he was here John could tell you) but suddenly we'd be in the middle of a track and John would just start crying or screaming — which freaked us out at the beginning. But we were always open to whatever anyone was going through so we just got on with it.

And it's good to know, we were 'the youngest bores of the year' and this card's pretty boring too. But anyway, thank you John and Yoko. And also, he still hasn't quite learnt how to spell my name. But hey! It's a pity the stamp's over one of the little drawings.

1970. My first wife Maureen and I had no problem moving homes. We went from Sunny Heights in Weybridge to Peter Sellers' place in Elstead, back to Sunny Heights and then to Round Hill. We made four complete house moves within 18 months. And Zak was a kid – he was only a baby then – 'Are we going to stay here?' he'd ask. And then in '73 – three years later, we went to Tittenhurst.

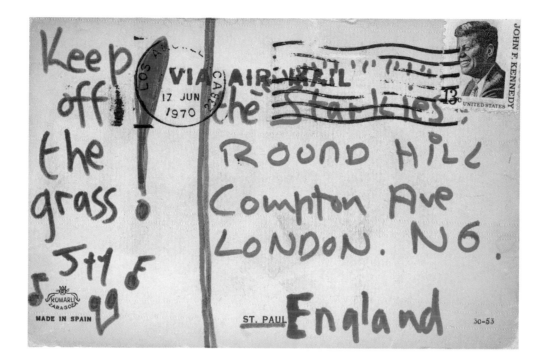

This is just after viewing the *Let It Be* film for the first time. I didn't like it that
much when I first saw it. It was too much into the discussions of John and Paul.
There was the interesting bit on the day George had left and we just started
playing like mad people. That's how we dealt with this crisis within the band.

I also wrote a song called 'Early 1970' which was all about the other three and
about what was happening. 'Pattie was in the garden picking daisies for George's
soup and when he comes to town, I know he's going to play with me.' 'John was
in bed eating cookies but when he comes to town, I know he's going to play with
me.' 'Paul lives on a farm – he's got plenty of sheep, or something, but when he
comes to town I wonder if he'll play with me.'

So, 'Keep off the grass!' OKAY!

For Auld Lang Syne.

Here's to you !
Many a happy day,
Many a sun-lit way,
And ever a Friend to say,
Here's to you !

Paul and Linda have had another child at this point and they must have got their place in Scotland by now. This was sent when I was just about to start recording with John and Yoko for their *Plastic Ono* LP. That was a great session: Klaus, John and me. It rocked. John was in a good space. It was recorded at EMI. We did two albums – John's album and Yoko's album – alongside each other.
Eric [Clapton] played on it too.

I remember Eric, Klaus, John and me were jamming at one point – and we're playing for 20 minutes waiting for Yoko, who was in the sound-proof booth with the cans and the mike, to join in. There was a lot of free expression music and it was one of those all-time great jams and then 20 minutes in she opens the door and says, 'Are you ready yet?' And we stopped and we never got up to that groove again! Phil Spector was around.

It's interesting that the apartment I had in Montague Square was where John and Yoko got together – they stayed there first and Jimi Hendrix stayed after them. And then I had the house in Weybridge where John and Yoko then went to live and then we ended up in Tittenhurst which they lived in too. It was just like musical chairs.

This was when he was doing *Self Portrait*, you know his manhood rising film. We just drove over one day to visit and he's standing there with his camera crew. He couldn't get it up and Yoko's there going, 'Jooooohn! Jooooohn!'
He got it up in the end.

Nashville. This was when I was making *Beaucoup Of Blues*. George was doing his
All Things Must Pass album and he flew Pete Drake over to perform on it. I think
he must have heard about him or knew him from Bob [Dylan]. I sent my car to
pick up Pete Drake and I had all these country tapes in there and we were talking
and he said, 'Oh, you like country music.' I said, 'I *love* country music.' So he said,
'You must come to Nashville and do an album,' I replied, 'Oh, I'm not going to
live in Nashville for six months.' He said, 'Six months! *Nashville Skyline* took two
days.' So I said, 'Okay, I'll come to Nashville and let's see what happens.'

H-9241
LANI rests after a strenuous Hawaiian songfest with the ukulele.
Photo by Chester Lau

We're alive
and living in
L.A!
tried to call
you in Nashville
– send me a copy
will ya?
love John + Yoko

Post Card

The Starceys
Round Hill
Compton Ave No.
LONDON
ENGLAND
U.K.

From 10 o'clock to 1 o'clock we'd listen to a lot of tracks by other writers, pick five tracks and then go in the studio in the afternoon and record them. And the next day, we'd listen to other songs, pick another five tracks and then in the afternoon we'd record them. It was all over by 8 o'clock at night. I'd written one called 'Coochy Coochy'. I wanted to play guitar because Pete had bought George and me guitars as gifts. So I was playing this incredible Harmony guitar and I went to this band of Nashville professionals and said, 'I've written this song and it's in E.' Only E – it didn't go anywhere. Anyway, we played it and it turned out fine. So in the end it was a fast experience but I ended up in a cupboard for several minutes hiding because everyone in Nashville decided to come and meet the Fab Ringo. That kind of thing was a drag then but it's not anymore.

Postcard 27 {front}

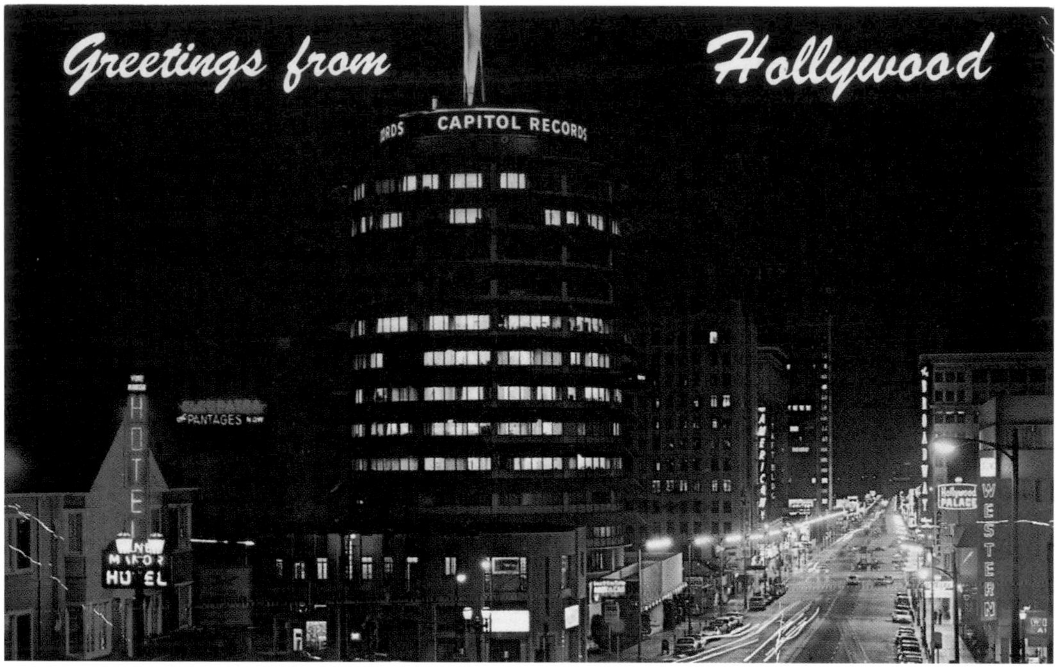

GLAMOUROUS HOLLYWOOD, CALIF.
Spectacular nite view of the famous "Round" Capitol Record Building and sparkling "Vine St." in the heart of the movie capitol of the world.

P59837

POST CARD

Plastichrome by COLOURPICTURE PUBLISHERS, INC., Boston 30, Mass., U.S.A.
DISTRIBUTED BY MITOCK & SONS, 7410 GREENBUSH AVE. NORTH HOLLYWOOD, CALIF.

Color by Carlo Marino

wish you here JtY. xx

Ringo + Mo
Round Hill
Compton Ave
N. 6. LONDON
ENGLAND
U.K.

No date. The sentiment is nice though.

Dear R. and M. et al

Doing nothing at all,
The sea-slug has lived
For eighteen thousand years.
∴
The slow days
Echoes heard
In a corner of Kyōto

love

PICTURE CARD

The Starrs
ROUND HILL
Compton Ave.
N.6
ENGRAND
U.K.

This is when John and Yoko were in Japan and John was meeting Yoko's parents for the first time before returning to London to join George and me to do battle with Paul in the High Court. How sad it all ended.

Hollywood. They're in LA now. Well, who knows where they are because we all
used to carry cards around and post them from different places.

I think, 'Who'd have thought it would come to this...' referred to the battle in the
High Court with Paul. This was a hell time because it was the family break-up.
Paul and John both had definite ideas of where things should be going and
George and I picked our side really for all our own reasons. That's what happened.
When you look back at stuff like that, hey, that's life! Things happen. How big is
the big picture? Everyone dials in on that year but what about the eight years
before or the first five years before it got messy? But the music didn't get messy.

I think that's about the life-span of a band anyway – eight years – because you grow up with the other band members. I joined at 22 and by 1970, aged 30, I had three kids. I had other priorities. I loved to play. I always loved to play and I always put all my energy into that but I wanted to go home at night. I didn't want to be just hanging out with the boys anymore. I wanted to see my kids grow up a little. We would spend a long time in the studio, but in all honesty the other three would spend more time than I did because I never got involved with the mixing. I would say, 'How do the drums sound? or 'I love that' or 'Where do you put my drums?' And that was all. The rest they would do because they wrote the songs.

Happy Xmas (war is over), Love, John & Yoko.

The movie 200 *Motels* had just opened at this time. That was great. Frank Zappa came to this house – Compton Avenue, Round Hill. I think someone in the office said, 'Frank wants to talk to you. He's got this idea for a movie and he wants you to play a part.' So I said, 'Well, send him over. We'll have tea and talk about it.'

So he came and laid out a huge music score. I can't read music. There was no script, just the music score. So I said, 'Sure! I've got to do it now!' I played *him* in the movie in the acting parts and *he* was the musician. So it was good.

66

*Happy Xmas.
to you 'n'
yours.
frae.*

Jocks 'n' Yous.

*The Strawelies.
Round Hill
Compton AVE.
London N 6
ENGLAND*

Air Mail

It was shot in England – Pinewood maybe. One of those places where you have to get up in the morning and go to. Frank was such a nice man. Because of the image which he put out, people were a bit afraid of him – this weird Frank Zappa – but he was just a very nice guy and loved his music. The whole joke of the movie was that I would record the band members talking – I was like the devil guy – and put it to music and force them to play it. So the premise was a lot of fun and it's always good hanging out with musicians.

John Lennon 1971

Spring evening 1879. *National Museum of Fine Arts, Budapest*.

Dear hello Ringo and MORE-REEN
thanx a lot for coming to
my birthday chaos, looks
like some good things will come
from the Museum show too!
lots of love to you and yours
love bonnie John + Yogurt
hello Maureen!! ♥ ♥
MRS. Lennon and her husband

I'll name that flute player in two notes.

This is from the McCartneys. Another one who didn't quite learn how to spell my name. 'Paul and Linda, kids and company', so they must have been with other people. It had to be a very narrow window of time because we weren't at Tittenhurst long. From '73 to '75.

1974. Maureen and I weren't divorced. I think I was living on my own.

I like tropical islands. I love the Caribbean. I'm not excited when you have to put
a big overcoat on.

I'm in Haslam Terrace now so it had to be from '74, '75 through '78. All these houses, all these homes. I was California dreaming. At 2am, because LA closed down at that time of night, you could hear all the traffic coming to my house. There was a party every night. John Bonham would always get a bee in his bonnet. Wherever he was in LA, he would drive up to my house, grab me and throw me in the pool.

Day or night – he wouldn't care. I'd be ready, about to go out and, 'No John, no!' 'No, I'm going to throw you in the pool!' He was a very good guy – well, for a while, and then he sadly left us.

This house was so great – I was doing the movie *Sextette*, with Mae West, and I had a party and there were about a hundred people at this party – including Mae. We had The Band and a lot of musicians and rock'n'rollers were there obviously. And Mae just sat in the corner in a big chair and all these rockers were on their knees to her because she was just so great. She had such a huge personality and she could mix with the best of them.

This is from George and Olivia in Hawaii – what a great shot. It's actually a home-made shot of their shadows. It's cool. This was at Woodrow Wilson when I lived in Los Angeles in '78. This was the house that burnt down.

It was when I was doing my television special *Ognir Rrats* and George came to play a part. But before he arrived he had an accident on a mountain in Maui. He'd fallen on his face but he still came because that was what he was like.

This is incredible because in those days you could only show African ladies' breasts – that was okay. You couldn't show white ladies' breasts – that wasn't okay. I visited John on and off if I was in New York. This was '79 but I don't know what I was doing in New York at that time. If we were in the same town we always used to hook up. If he came to Los Angeles (I spent a lot of time in LA) we'd hook up too. It was no big deal. The next time I went was 1980 and it was all over.

`Wild Goose`
(yippie aye aye)!
great
disco

ZULU WATER-CARRIERS — Natal
Village maidens in the Valley of a Thousand Hills carrying
their "Ukhamba" (clay pots) homeward.
ZOELOE WATERDRAERS — Natal
Meisies van 'n stat in die Vallei van 'n Duisend Heuwels dra
hul "Ukhamba" (kleipotte) huis toe.

Richard Starkey
Woodrow Wilson Drive
Hollywood
90046.
CALIFORNIA.

I love LA. I just love it. It has so much for me, and after all these years of having a
home there we have a lot of friends and now we have family there. I love the
weather and I love the lifestyle.

I love Monte Carlo too because my ideal was, 'I'll live anywhere with a palm tree,'
and there aren't many of them in Liverpool. I love the sun. Even in the days when
I wasn't taking too much notice of the weather, it was better to be in a warm
climate for me.

I'd just been in Denmark and I actually played on Cat Stevens' record because he was there too. And he wiped me off! I mean, I can't blame him because around those years, I was losing control! It's funny because you cop such a resentment at the time: 'What! He wiped me off!' God knows what I played for him.

'Why tell Paul Drew and not you!?' Then it probably meant something completely different. Wasn't he a DJ?

The Great Wall of China – John was moving about and sometimes he moved on his own. Yoko used to send him away on his own so he'd grow up. I don't know if he grew up but he certainly went places without her. And I think he had a very strange time in Macao if my memory serves me well.

The other three all had a head start in German because they'd taken it in school.
It was like the second language class. You had to learn it. I got quite good in my
way in Hamburg because I wanted to eat. The first German I learnt was the word
for 'cornflakes' and Stu Sutcliffe took me to this Chinese restaurant that did
pfannkuchen – pancakes – and they were like eight inches thick with lemon and
sugar. They filled you up. And they were cheap. We weren't getting a lot of
money then. This was when I was with Rory and Stu was with The Beatles. So all
the words we learnt were the ones we needed to survive. And then all the waiters
would teach you how to swear at somebody without you knowing it. So I'd be
calling people 'dogs' or 'pigs' and they would be grabbing me, 'Don't call me
that!' And the waiters used to think it was great fun.

to Richard und "Bars" fröhlicher Gebürtstag von alle de gang

...schutz

George, Olivia and Dhani

wish you a

Very Happy New Year

1927. ————————→ 1827 : Hello.

But in the end we'd pick up the language by travelling by bus and taxi and living with German girls. Now wherever you go, everyone speaks English and wherever we stay there's always assistance. That's that anyway.

Great memories of the Friar Park home. I don't understand what '1927 – 1827' means though. Some of it only made sense on the day. Twelve hours later nobody knew what the hell we were talking about. I've got notebooks of things I wrote. You'd need a Martian to decipher them now.

We only had an in-tray in our office. Barbara and I would get up and drive to our office in London and we'd go back to bed when we got there. We'd eventually get down into the office with Joan, my PA, and she'd say, 'Well, this needs an answer.' 'Give it to me next week,' I'd reply. 'This needs an answer too.' 'Next time,' I'd say and so we'd keep the in-tray going and nothing would reach the out-tray. And then we'd make great decisions like, 'Let's go to Iceland!'

This is when I first lived in Monte Carlo in the mid-Seventies through the early Eighties. I went there for all those good reasons. Three things happened in the first couple of years in Monte Carlo. One, I went mad and spent a lot of time – it seems like years now – hanging out with John Bonham, who spent a year there. Two, I shaved my head and every hair on my face and the third was that part of my intestines closed down and I was in a lot of pain. I got to the hospital finally and they gave me a shot of pain killer. Then, when I felt some relief I said, 'Oh. I can go now.' And Professor Chatalin, the doctor who was taking care of me, said, 'Yes, you can go. And you can die!' So I said, 'Well maybe we should have the operation.'

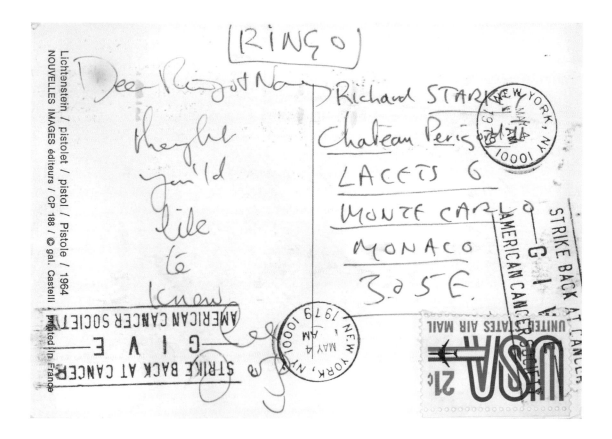

They took five feet of my intestines out. I was in intensive care for five days and in a recovery ward for a week and then I conned my way out a couple of days later to go and live in the Hôtel de Paris because I hate hospitals – I spent two years in them when I was a boy. I used to sit in the bar at the Hôtel de Paris. I couldn't drink because my intestines were healing but I could hang out with people so it helped get over that low passage. I'd given up cigarettes and I started lighting them for people because it gave me a buzz. One day I smoked a whole cigarette and within a week I'd bought a carton and was back on 60 a day. It was far out. Anyway, I don't smoke now and I recommend it to all of you reading this book.

Later that month I was at Eric and Pattie Clapton's wedding. That was a really good day except that Ronnie Lane was there and he had just found out that he had multiple sclerosis. I said, 'Hey Ronnie. How are you doing?' He said, 'I'm melting.'

Zak and Jim Capaldi were playing drums because Eric had a band set up on stage. I have fond memories of that day.

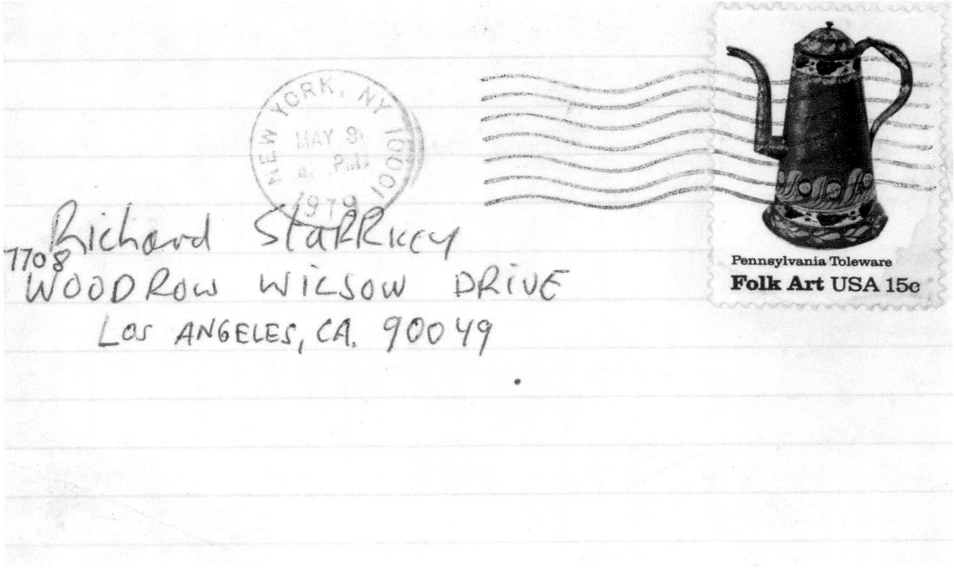

NEW YORK, NY 10001
MAY 9
1979
Richard Starkey
7708 WOODROW WILSON DRIVE
LOS ANGELES, CA. 90049
Pennsylvania Toleware
Folk Art USA 15c

"HOW IT
ITi
THE
MOON"
(WITH FEMALE
VOCAL HARMONY)
DISCO-NATCH!

BLONDIES'
HEART OF GLASS
IS THE TYPE
OF STUFF
Y'ALL SHOULD
DO —
GREAT + SIMPLE

← i KNOW, THIS AIN'T SIMPLE
i KNOW

This is John telling me what sort of things to record – he used to say, 'Do this sort of track.' 'Do it in a disco style!' He'd obviously just heard Blondie's 'Heart of Glass' which we all loved – that was a really cool record. Debbie Harry's a very nice woman. In '79 my career was heading for hell anyway. It went from the success of the records I'd made from 1971 up to the peak in 1974 with the *Ringo* album, which John was on and the *Goodnight Vienna* album, which was John's song, to starting to turn to hell. I was taking less and less interest. I was more interested in just being out of my head. The point of the card is, it didn't matter what people's perceptions of us were, you can see from these cards that there's still a lot of contact, a lot of thought. The relationship never went away.

LOOKING TOWARDS THE CORAL REEF FROM A WHITE SAND
BEACH, SHADED BY COCONUT PALMS   JAMAICA W.I.

This is somewhere between '81 and '87. They loved Jamaica – they were always going there. I went several times and I loved it too. The last time I went it felt too dangerous, but the times before were great. We'd take the kids.

Burning Spear was my favourite. Bob [Marley] was great too. I never met him but he might prove me wrong.

TASMANIAN DEVIL
This thickly set and often vicious animal is found only in Tasmania. It is approximately 75 cm. long and 22 cm. high when fully grown. This marsupial is a powerful animal and preys on most bush and mountain animals.

Hi Pals - we're in Tassa' for a while & its a very nice. Hope the sessions went o.k, Everyone is in Aussie. Reg + Gerry to name ② See you later - love George Harris & Dhani Boy 32" +.

Mr & Mrs R&B. Starkey.
TITENHURST PARK
ASCOT. .
BERKSHIRE
ENGLAND.
U.K.

DS 371
Colour Photography and Copyright by Robert Schorn.
Printed in Australia

Published by Douglas Souvenir Distributors - Tasmania
(004) 312806

Australia 35c
SOUTHERN RIGHT WHALE

The session George is referring to is for the *Old Wave* album. 'Reg' is Elton John and 'Gerry' is ?

1981 was the first year that Barbara and I settled down in Tittenhurst. It was nice and we'd just upgraded the studio there. We had a lot of fun. When I left the country for Monaco in 1976 I turned the house into a studio with accommodation for the bands. When Barbara and I came there in '81 we had two German Shepherds who didn't like anybody except the family and when we returned we'd hear screaming. The guitarists would want to go out and get some fresh air and you'd hear barking and see a lot of musicians up trees. Those dogs would rip your clothes off.

THE GREAT BARRIER REEF.
North Queensland.
Green Turtles mating. Three really is a crowd with these Green Turtles. The bottom reptile is a female, the other two are courting males.
Photo: Ron & Valerie Taylor

Box 1045, Cairns, Qld., 4870, Ph. 51-4935

Printed in Australia

PEER productions

PCO 445

BENNETT'S NUDIBRANCH

55c AUSTRALIA

Hello R + B.
a little turtle groupage
from the Barrier Reef.
See you in July?
Lots of love
George Olivia
& Dhani.

Mr & Mrs R. Starkey.
TITTENHURST PARK.
SUNNINGHILL/ASCOT
LONDON ROAD.
BERKSHIRE
ENGLAND. U.K.

© Copyright 1982

Back to the Barrier Reef. Turtles humping. George was another one who liked hot weather. He loved Friar Park too and all he did to it.

The Eighties were woah! I was given Tittenhurst Park in a re-shuffle of Apple in the Seventies so I first moved in there in '73 with Maureen and the kids but by '75 the marriage was over. So I just kept it and turned it into a studio. Bands like Whitesnake went and recorded there. And when Barbara and I got together and married we stopped letting it out and kept it for ourselves.

To Ring, Bar
and Kids.
Lots of love
from Paul Lin,
Stell, and James
on their sunny hols!
♡ love ya.

SAGUARO CACTUS AND RAINBOW. This is
a most unusual scene since very seldom is there
rain in the desert.
B12821-Color Photo: Ray Manley

R+B STARKEY
TITTENHURST
PARK
ASCOT.

NR. LONDON.
ENGLAND.

Published by Petley Studios
4051 E. Van Buren, Phoenix, AZ. 85008

Of course John made 'Imagine' there and that's our living room with the big white piano in it on the album cover. We also made the record *Old Wave* with Joe Walsh at Tittenhurst. Joe and I were old pals so I called him to come over and produce it, which he did. We were both a little more reckless in those days! There was one interesting night when Joe felt we should have a party for a few hours. How he could put a time limit on it I have no idea but anyway, it went on for more than the hours we wanted and we didn't get much done that day. But we had loads of fun – there were a lot of British musicians on the record and we finished it in Los Angeles.

Dear Richard & Barbara,

Just another typical sight along the Hana Highway. The Hawaiians are real "laid back" as you can see. Wiki Wiki! Love Livy, George & Diane

South Seas Island Men

HONOLULU, Hawaiian Resources Co. Ltd. • 1123 Kapahulu Ave. • Honolulu, HI 96816

Mr. & Mrs Starkey
Tittenhurst Park
London Road
Sunninghill near
Ascot
England

I took Barbara to Venice in Easter of 1984 and we spent a lot of hours in the jacuzzi in the Cipriani. But I was determined that we should see the Bridge of Sighs so we walked over it. We never got into a gondola I'm afraid. We decided we'd go on the Orient Express, that we'd go into Venice and have a holiday. We didn't know it was Easter and that every family in the world was on holiday then and that they all had cameras. But, the interesting thing was that on the train there was this very weird guy from Brazil with a white military aspect suit and his daughter, Heidi. They were like old Nazis on the run.

A very strange couple.

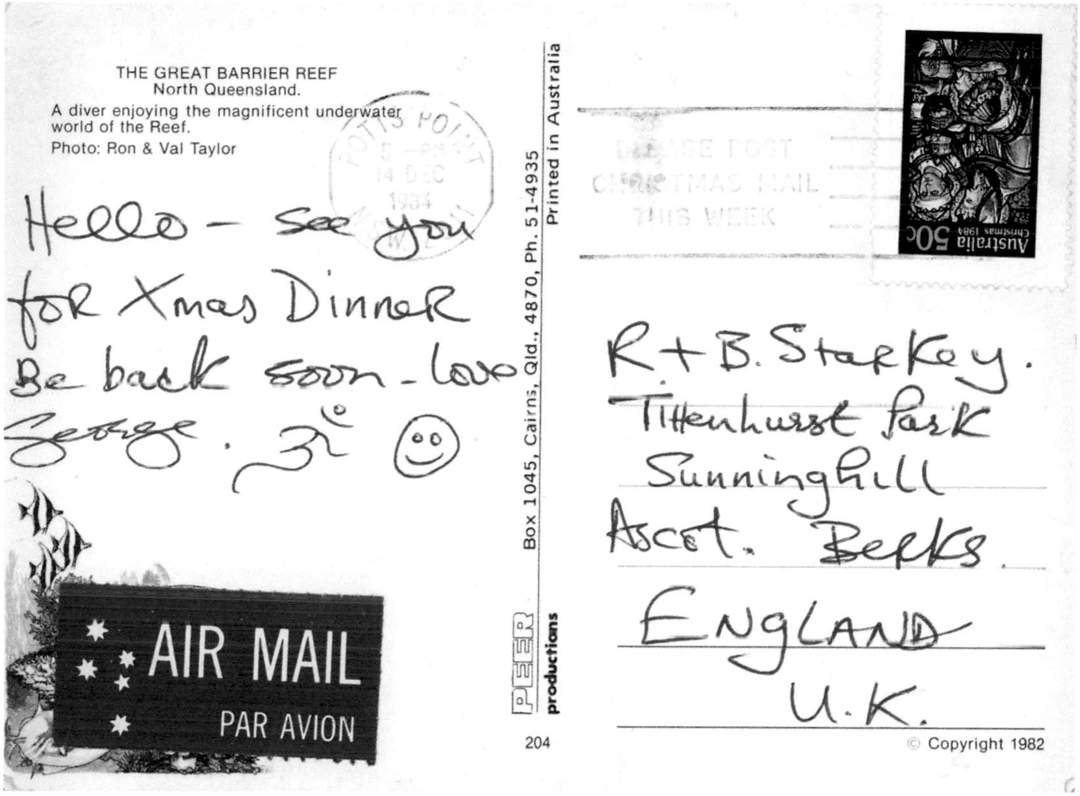

THE GREAT BARRIER REEF
North Queensland.
A diver enjoying the magnificent underwater
world of the Reef.
Photo: Ron & Val Taylor

Hello – see you
for Xmas Dinner
Be back soon – love
George. 🕉 ☺

R + B. Starkey.
Tittenhurst Park
Sunninghill
Ascot. Berks.
ENGLAND
U.K.

AIR MAIL
PAR AVION

This is from George after he helped Derek [Taylor] launch *Fifty Years Adrift* in
Sydney. Barbara and I went to Heron Island, which you can walk round in like 20
minutes. It's on the Barrier Reef. What can I say – it's incredible.

This was just after the *Artists United Against Apartheid* LP

That was with Little Stevie Van Zandt and I got Zak, my son, to play on it too.
That was the thrill – I *was* against apartheid but it was also important to me
because it was the first time that Zak and I participated together in a project.

CAMPBELTOWN—Main Street

6023

Campbeltown Main Street! That is just the worst card! But thank you anyway. In 1986 I was heading for the downfall of '88. God bless 'em – they kept sending the cards.

I went and played with the Beach Boys around this time which I have no memory of either but somebody showed me a photo so I know it must have happened. 'Oh okay, I was there.' Brian [Wilson] was great – he was on my album *Vertical Man* – and he'd come in and he'd sing a part and say, 'Okay, give me another track' and he'd sing another part. 'Okay, give me another track.' He was the only one who had the completed piece in his head and he'd say, 'Okay, let's go – put it all on,' and it was incredible.

Dear Rich,
Barb, +
kiddie widdies!
love from the
Sun. 90
and no complaints!
Paul, Lin + kids

RINGO + BARB,
℅
TITTENHURST
PARK.
ASCOT.
BERKSHIRE.
ENGLAND

LONDON ROAD

TUCSON AZ
PM
3 NOV
1987

HELP GOODWILL
HELP
THE HANDICAPPED

TRANSPACIFIC
AIRMAIL 1995
USAirmail 44

CACTI AND DESERT FLORA OF THE GREAT SOUTHWEST

K-341-C

Published and Distributed by Petley Studios, Inc.
4051 E. Van Buren, Phoenix, Arizona 85008

Paul and Linda in Tucson again. They had this house there that we could never mention. We know a lot of people in Arizona and Tucson and they'd all say, 'Oh Paul was here.' 'Oh no, don't tell them I've got a house here,' he'd say.

'90 degrees. No complaints'

In '87 I was heading for the last round-up and that was the thing with *All Things Must Pass* because George said, when he reissued it, 'You played on *All Things Must Pass* didn't you?' I wasn't sure and he didn't know either until he got involved in the credits – 'And my old mate Ringo who doesn't remember plays on three-quarters of the record.'

Skiing – I love skiing. I didn't start until I was 50 and now I'm up and down any mountain you can throw me on. We go every year to Colorado. It's just the best there is. You're in the mountains and everything's white – it's a spiritual situation just to be up there. Some days the mountain's really quiet and there's not a lot of traffic. I've had several really incredible moments from just being up there.

V A T U L E L E
I S L A N D   R E S O R T

Glynde Mews – into the Nineties. Barbara and I went to Fiji a lot. 'Bula' is like, 'Hi, how are you doing?' We used to go to this island and I'd scream, 'Bula! Cognac!' and the waiter would bring me cognac and sometimes he'd swim with a bottle of it up to our little hut. Later I went back sober and one of the guys shouted, 'Bula! Cognac!' I was like, 'No! Not today thank you!'

† VATULELE
ISLAND RESORT

BULA! OUR feet
are getting bigger every
day. Oli's are about size
23 - and mine - 27 -
we still have a way to
to to size 29 but then we
still have another 9 weeks
holiday l l l l love G+O

VATULELE ISLAND RESORT
WORLDWIDE RESERVATIONS
SYDNEY AUSTRALIA
TEL (61) (2) 326 1055   Fax (61) (2) 327 2764
NORTH AMERICA
800-828 9146   Fax (310) 338 0708

RELAIS &
CHATEAUX.

AFFIX
STAMP
HERE

R. + B. Starkey
4 Glynde Mews
London SW3 1LJ
England

And their feet are so big. The Fijians have their feet on the ground. Just one of those things. I love the Fijians. I don't know what it's like on the main island but on the smaller islands it was always really mellow because they'd be drinking kava and playing guitars.

I wonder if this is the place where Billy Connolly got married – Billy and Pam. Looks like their doorway actually.

ACKNOWLEDGMENTS

We would like to thank Staffan Olander for his research and Diana LeCore for preparing the index.
This book would not be possible without the thoughtfulness of John, Paul and George in sending the cards in the first place or of course without Ringo for kindly allowing them to be published. So, a sincere 'thank you' is sent to the Fab Four and to their nearest and dearest.

All reasonable effort has been made to find and contact the photographers and copyright owners of the images printed in this publication. Any omissions or errors are inadvertent and will be corrected in subsequent editions, provided notification is sent to the publisher.

Image credits: front cover – Nick Roylance (Ringo) and Torbjörn Ehrnvall, Åhlén & Åkerlund Förlag (Paul, George & John);
page 2 – The Sean O'Mahony Collection.

Postcards: Ashleigh Brilliant, www.ashleighbrilliant.com (*Pot Shots No.34*); Camera Press, London (*Prince Charles*, photograph by Godfrey Argent); Estate of Roy Lichtenstein/DACS 2004 (*Pistol 1964*); Frederick Warne & Co. Ltd (*Mr Jeremy Fisher*, illustration by Beatrix Potter); Grant L. Robertson Inc (*New Orleans Street Car*, photograph by Grant Robertson); Grønlund/Fotodanmark.dk (*Copenhagen, Denmark*); Kardorama Ltd (*Coldstream Guard, Windsor Castle*); Whiteholme Ltd (*Campbeltown High Street*).

Figures in italics indicate postmarks on postcards.

200 Motels (film) 66-7
All Things Must Pass 58, 106
Altman, Robert 45
Apple 94
Arizona 105
Artists United Against Apartheid 101
Asher, Jane 16
Aspinall, Neil 8
Athens 45
Australia 91, 93
Austria 45

Band, The 75
Barbados 45
Beach Boys 103
Beatles, The
  break-up of 34, 63
  George leaves 31, 53
  meeting at Brookfields 31
  relationship continues after band break-up 87
  Ringo walks out 25
Beaucoup Of Blues 58
Beverly Hills, California 59
Blondie 87
Bonham, John 74-5, 84
Brown, Peter 44
Burning Spear 89

California 74
Campbeltown, Argyll 11, 55, 103, 103
Capaldi, Jim 85
Caribbean 73
Cavern, The, Liverpool 8
Charles, HRH The Prince of Wales 41
Chatalin, Professor 84
China, Great Wall of 81
Clapton, Eric 55, 85
Clapton, Pattie (Pattie Boyd) 85
Colorado 107
Connolly, Billy 109
'Coochy Coochy' 59

Denmark 45, 45, 80
Drake, Pete 58, 59
Drew, Paul 81
Dylan, Bob 58

Early 1970' 53
Elizabeth II, Queen 21, 47
Elstead, Surrey ('Brookfields', Cutt Mill Lane) 31, 51
EMI 55
Esher, Surrey 10
Evans, Mal 8

Farrow, Mia 16
Fifty Years Adrift 99
Fiji 108-9
Finland 45
Friar Park, Henley-on-Thames, Berkshire 83, 93, 101

Germany 45
Glynde Mews, south west London 108
Goodnight Vienna 87
Great Barrier Reef, Australia 93, 93, 99
Greece 45, 47

Hamburg 82
Hampstead Heath, London 10
Harrison, George
  accident in Maui 77
  All Things Must Pass 58, 106
  annoyed by Paul at Twickenham 31
  Australia 91, 93, 99, 99
  break-up of the band 63, 64
  Drake's guitar gift 59
  in Esher 10
  Hawaii 77, 77, 97
  Henley-on-Thames home (Friar Park) 93, 101
  I Me Mine 44
  in India 16, 17
  is asked to return to the band 31
  leaves the band 31, 53
  Ognir Rrats (television special) 77
  Vatulele Island Resort, Fiji 109
Harrison, Olivia 77
Harry, Debbie 87
Haslam Terrace, Sunset Plaza Drive, Hollywood 74
'Heart of Glass' 87
Hendrix, Jimi 57
Henley-on-Thames (Friar Park) 83, 93, 101
Heron Island, Great Barrier Reef 99
Highgate, London 48
Hollywood, California 61, 64
Honolulu, Hawaii 75, 97
Hopkin, Mary 35
Hotel Cipriani, Venice 97
Hôtel de Paris, Monte Carlo 85

I Me Mine 44
Iceland 83
'Imagine' 95
India 15, 16, 17

Jamaica 89, 89

Janov, Dr Arthur 48
Japan 63, 63, 65, 75, 81
Joan (Ringo's PA) 83
John, Elton 91
Jones, Brian 17
Jones, Quincy 35

Lane, Ronnie 85
Las Vegas 35
Lennon, Cynthia 10, 13, 16
Lennon, John
  Beverly Hills 59
  Bonfire Night at Ringo's 11
  break-up of the band 63, 64
  China, Great Wall of 81
  Denmark 45
  Greece 47
  Hollywood 61
  India 15, 15, 16, 17
  Japan 63, 63, 65, 75, 81
  in *Let It Be* 53
  Los Angeles 51
  makes 'Imagine' 95
  Marrakesh, Morocco 13, 13
  New York City 57, 57, 67, 78, 85, 86
  Plastic Ono LP 55
  and Primal Scream concept 48-9
  on *Ringo* album 87
  in St George's Hill, Weybridge 10
  Scotland 43
  Self Portrait 57
  sends back his MBE 47
  at Tittenhurst 57
  Tobago 13
  Tokyo 63, 65
  Tywyn, Merioneth 41
  Yoko sends him away on his own 81
Lennon, Julian 10, 11
Let It Be (film) 53
Liverpool 35, 79
Los Angeles 51, 64, 74, 78, 79, 95

Macao 81
McCartney, Linda 9, 37, 55, 71, 105
McCartney, Sir Paul
  annoys George at Twickenham 31
  break-up of the band 63, 64
  Campbeltown, Argyll 11, 55, 103, 103
  home in Scotland 55
  in India 16, 17
  in *Let It Be* 53
  Martinique 73
  Maussane-les-Alpilles, 19

Montego Bay, Jamaica 89
Nassau, Bahamas 33
New Orleans 71
Portugal 37
and Ringo's return to the band 25
St John's Wood, London 25, 29, 31
Spain 9
Switzerland 107
Tucson, Arizona 95, 105, 105
The Magic Christian (film) 19
Maharishi Yogi 16, 17
Marley, Bob 89
Marrakesh, Morocco 13
Martha (dog) 22
Martin, Sir George 34, 35
Martinique 73
Maui, Hawaii 77
Maussane-les-Alpilles, France 19
Monaco 91
Montague Square, New York City 57
Monte Carlo 79, 84
Montego Bay, Jamaica 89

Nashville 58, 59
Nashville Skyline 58
Nassau, Bahamas 33
New Brighton, Merseyside 43
New Orleans 71
New York City 57, 57, 67, 78, 86
Nilsson, Harry 45
North Wales 43

'Octopus's Garden' 15
Ognir Rrats (television special) 77
Old Wave album 91, 95
Ono, Yoko
  at Tittenhurst 57
  in Japan 63
  in New York City 57
  Plastic Ono LP 55
  and Primal Scream concept 48
  and *Self Portrait* 57
  sends John away on his own 81
Orient Express 97

Pinewood Studios 67
Plastic Ono Band 55
Portugal 37
Presley, Elvis 35
Primal Scream concept 48

Ringo 87
Rishikesh, India 16, 17
Round Hill, Compton Avenue, London 51, 66

St John's Wood, London 25, 29, 31
Sardinia 15
Saville Row, London 39, 44
Scotland 43, 43, 55
Seaforth, Merseyside 43
Self Portrait (film) 57
Sellers, Peter 15, 19, 51
Sentimental Journey 34
Sextette (film) 75
Spector, Phil 55
Spinetti, Victor 13
Starkey, Barbara (Ringo's second wife) 83, 91, 94, 97, 99
Starkey, Jason 16
Starkey, Lee 41
Starkey, Maureen (Ringo's first wife) 9, 10, 13, 16, 51, 73, 94
Starkey, Zak
  Artists United Against Apartheid 101
  childhood 8, 10, 11, 51
  plays drums at Clapton's wedding 85
Starr, Ringo
  in *200 Motels* 66-7
  and *All Things Must Pass* 106
  Artists United Against Apartheid 101
  on the band's break-up 64-5
  Bonfire Night 11
  break-up of the band 63
  childhood trips 43
  Clapton's wedding 85
  country album 35, 58-9
  cycling in Wales 43
  downfall of 1988 103
  Drake's guitar gift 59
  at Elstead 31, 51
  end of marriage to Maureen 73, 94
  Fiji holidays 108-9
  at Glynde Mews 108
  Goodnight Vienna album 87
  in Hamburg 82
  Heron Island 99
  I Me Mine 44
  in India 16, 17
  intestinal operation 84-5
  on *Let It Be* 53
  Los Angeles 77, 78, 79
  love of skiing 107
  makes *Beaucoup Of Blues* 58
  marries Barbara 94
  Monte Carlo 79, 84
  moves to Highgate 48
  moves to Monaco (1976) 91
  in New York 57, 78
  Ognir Rrats (television special) 77
  Old Wave 91, 95

Plastic Ono LP 55
Ringo album 87
  at Round Hill 51, 66
  Sardinia holiday 15
  and *Sentimental Journey* 34
  in *Sextette* 75
  on smoking 85
  at Tittenhurst 51, 57, 71, 91, 94
  Tobago holiday with John 13
  in Venice (1984) 97
  Vertical Man album 103
  walks out on the band 25
  at Weybridge (1965) 8, 9, 10, 15, 51, 57
Stephenson, Pamela (Mrs Connolly) 109
Stevens, Cat 80
Stills, Stephen 19
Storm, Rory 82
Sunderland, Tyne & Wear 43
'Sunny Heights' see Weybridge, Surrey
Sutcliffe, Stu 82
Sweden 45
Switzerland 107
Sydney, Australia 99

Taylor, Derek 99
Tittenhurst Park, Sunninghill, near Ascot, Berkshire
  Ringo's home 51, 57, 71, 94
  studio 91, 94, 95
Tobago 13
Tokyo, Japan 63, 65
Tucson, Arizona 95, 105, 105
Twickenham Studios 31
200 Motels (film) 66-7
Tywyn, Merioneth 41

Van Zandt, Little Stevie 101
Vatulele Island Resort, Fiji 109
Venice 97
Vertical Man 103
Voormann, Klaus 55

Wales 16, 17, 43
Walsh, Joe 93
West, Mae 75
Weybridge, Surrey ('Sunny Heights', St George's Hill) 8, 9, 10, 15, 51, 57
White Album 25
Whitesnake 94
Wilson, Brian 103
Woodrow Wilson Drive, Los Angeles 77

Zappa, Frank 66, 67